Domination in Christ

By

Dr. Kenton Edward Emmanuel Connor

TABLE OF CONTENT

COPYRIGHT

In no way is it legal to reproduce, duplicate, or transmit any part of this document in either electronic means or in printed format. Recording of this publication is strictly prohibited and any storage of this document is not allowed unless with written permission from the publisher. All rights reserved.

The information provided herein is stated to be truthful and consistent, in that any liability, in terms of inattention or otherwise, by any usage or abuse of any policies, processes, or directions contained within is the solitary and utter responsibility of the recipient reader. Under no circumstances will any legal responsibility or blame be held against the publisher for any reparation, damages, or monetary loss due to the information herein, either directly or indirectly.

Respective authors own all copyrights not held by the publisher. The information herein is offered for informational purposes solely, and is universal as so. The presentation of the information is without contract or any type of guarantee assurance.

The trademarks that are used are without any consent, and the publication of the trademark is without permission or backing by the trademark owner. All trademarks and brands within this book are for clarifying purposes only and are the owned by the owners themselves, not affiliated with this document.

INTRODUCTION

Trends hit the Body from time to time and need to be discussed. The idea of "dominion" has been around quite awhile and has been discussed the entire time.

It's not all negative, you know. Dominion is a totally Scriptural idea. But because of translation issues, things have gotten a wee bit confused. Dominion has been intertwined with power, and authority, and even more, but sometimes improperly. Let's talk about the word itself.

"Dominion", "government", "rule", "lording over", these are all proper ways to translate the Greek words of the family "kurios." Jesus was called Kurios, "Lord" all His days here. He is the Lord, after all. His is the dominion. His the power. His the authority. The question before us is, how much of that authority and rule is passed on to His followers?

A word first about power and authority. Picture the policeman. This is not very

original, and I'm sure you've heard it many times, but it works. The policeman shows his authority by his badge and uniform. He shows his power by his weapons. Dominion, in this context, would be pretty hard for him to show, except that he represents the City or County magistrates and carries their ruler-ship.

The analogy breaks down - or rather holds up? - when the said policeman shows up at a Council meeting and tries to run the show. The real dominions present will make short work of him.

Those claiming the authority and power of Jesus have some pretty good legs to stand on. They can take authority over sickness, they can announce forgiveness of sin, they can cast out the devil's own servants, they can call for changes of nature and situation and... you name it. Pretty powerful folks, these believers.

It's when they start acting like they are running the show that Jesus Himself has to say, uh, excuse Me.

He warned His followers that they were in no way to exercise dominion (His very word) over the Gentiles or each other as the people of this world did and do. Verboden! Jude warns us not to despise dominions of any sort. Paul says that the powers that be are of God. Not for us to mess with. Paul also comments to the Corinthians that he in no way had dominion (again, his word!) over their faith.

So except where Jesus shows up in a "dominion" text, where it is all His, it is simply not owned by anyone else.

Dominion is closely related to, even synonymous with, the idea of "reigning." Here we find another piece of the puzzle for would-be dominion theologians. Reigning for believers is all in the future.

Sorry. There is a move afoot to grab all Millennial passages and bring them into our day. This is robbery of the worst sort. If you've been one to try to steal Christian hope, please stop. Without hope, all we have is the moment.

Would you believe, the full reign of even Jesus is also out there in the future? Hebrews 2:8 indicates that not everything that needs to be con□uered has been con□uered, as it will be in the Millennial rule of Jesus on earth. Those who want the Kingdom now are way ahead of the King! Some day we shall see all enemies put under his feet (I Corinthians 15:25), but that day is after He comes in judgment and sets up the fullness of the Kingdom that we are to preach.

Romans 5:17, II Timothy 2:12, Revelation 5:10. We shall reign with Christ if we suffer with Him now. The reigning as kings has not begun.

For now, it is that other Jesus we see. The one who bore our sorrows. The crucified but risen Jesus is the one we must preach. Not crucified alone, and left on a cross. Not resurrected alone, as though the cross is of no value or significance now. Indeed, a cross-less Christianity is nothing more than being a nice guy who does cool things.

Paul said to that American-style church in Corinth: You reigned as kings. But we didn't. We're happy for you, but we'll keep our profile low.

As disciples grow, they go lower. They don't try to take over, they try to give away. They don't try to dominate (dominion), they become slaves.

Dominion theology and Book of Acts reality are totally different creatures. Exercise your authority and power, but let Jesus be King!

THE SPIRIT OF DOMINION

THE SPIRIT OF DOMINION: is the Holy Spirit that empowers the totality of man to rule over the earth and life circumstances.

DOMINION: is the authority to rule, take charge, manage or control what is placed in your care.

THE 3 AREAS OF MAN'S DOMINION

1. DOMINION OVER THE EARTH
The earth is the solid part of the planet with everything within it. The animal kingdom, the plant kingdom and aquatic kingdom where subjected to mankind. The earth is God's property given to man to manage and explore. The secondary assignment of God for man was to rule the earth from the Garden of Eden. This was demonstrated by Adam in naming the animals and watering the plants, ensuring that everything made by God fulfills its purpose. God has put man in charge to manage the earth from the beginning. But when he fell from God's standards for

righteous compliance the devil took over the mandate of dominion of the earth from him. Man who was a legal occupant became a mere slave to the devil and all his manipulations when he surrendered this right rulership. Frankly, the Spirit of dominion which gives man power over God's property and Satan's strategy left him when fell. He was disconnected from the life of God (Spirit of dominion) and chased out of the place of fellowship with Him, but it was not yet over for him. Therefore, the fall of man was a fall from dominion mandate.

2. DOMINION OVER SATAN AND THE WORLD SYSTEM 1John 4:4-5

The devil and his cohorts are bodiless illegal beings on earth. Though were cast out by God from heaven to the earth as a result of their willful plot to ascend the place of God Almighty. As the devil didn't succeed in his carefully laid down plan to overthrow God in heaven; he automatically plotted this evil against man. God made man like Himself to be in charge over the earth knowing fully well that devil has come down here on earth to stay for a

while. Man was created to have dominion over Satan and his systematic influence in this world. But the devil took over the place of man by deception. However, when Jesus died on the cross and was buried and resurrected, He came up with a new kind of life and was raised by the Spirit of dominion that con□uers the devil and the worldly system. Therefore, whosoever, believes in the finished work of grace by Christ Jesus on the cross; receives the Spirit of dominion will execute his original mandate by God.

3. DOMINION OVER SIN, SICKNESS AND DEATH. Rom. 6:14
The kind of life that Adam inherited from God in the beginning; was a life that knew no sin and was not made subject to sickness and death; until Adam was disconnected from the Spirit of dominion. But thank God for the coming of the last Adam- Christ Jesus who has restored man to the place of dominion by the Holy Spirit. The power of sin is broken; sickness has been taken care by the stripes of Jesus. The death of Jesus on the cross has deprived death of its power and reveals its

futility over humanity. The problem of man is longer sin but ignorance of their redemptive rights in Christ Jesus.

HOW TO LIVE AND WALK IN DOMINION

1. YOU MUST BE BORN OF GOD 1John 5:1-5

The life of God is a supernatural life possessed by the natural man who has received Him. Being born of God is when the Holy Spirit has recreated the human spirit by the word of God. This rebirth is a spiritual phenomenon that is obtained by faith via the impartation of the Holy Spirit. It is also known as eternal life, being born again or regeneration. This kind of life helps you to live and walk in dominion in this world of sin. There is no natural man that can live above the law of sin and death that controls his actions and gives sin dominion over his life; except he submits to the law of the spirit of life in Christ Jesus.

2. YOU MUST LIVE AND WALK BY FAITH
2Cor. 5:7, Heb. 2:4, 10:36, 11:6, Rom. 1:17, Gal. 3:11

The Christian life is impossible without the operation of faith in the human spirit and the help of the Holy Spirit. The Bible says that the victory by which we overcome the world is our faith. Our faith is a spiritual re□uirement to excel in our Christian walk. To live by faith means that everything you do is an act of faith by being conscious of your spiritual state. And to walk by faith means to demonstrate your invisible believe in God in the visible world. In other words, living out your convictions and confessions in this world of confusion.

3. MAINTAIN A PRAYERFUL LIFE
Prayer is one the ways to exercise and maintain your dominion over the earth. The mission of Jesus didn't start until He took time to pray and to overcome He continued in prayers. The life of prayer is a life that empowers and emboldens your human spirit to soar above Satan and life circumstances. When we pray we commit God into the scene of our faced situations of life. Nothing changes until we decide to

change it on our knees. Sometimes, the most careless aspect of many Christians is usually their prayer life and devil seeks such an opening to launch an attack or reinforce against us.

4. RULE YOUR WORLD WITH GOD'S WORD.
Pro. 18:4; 20-21
The world from the beginning of creation was framed and still upheld by the word of God. It is with God's word that you can recreate your future and maintain your dominion over the world. There is no situation that God's word cannot change if only you can believe in the efficacy of His word and also confess it. Everything in life responds to what you say. The greatest power of humans lies in their thoughts and on their tongues. You are either saved, safe or enslaved by what you say.

RESTORATION OF THE DOMINION IMAGE OF GOD IN MAN

We all seek for prominence and identity in this life because we must understand that it is God who created us for this purpose. This purpose was the discussion that was on when God started to create men. The Bible reveals it by saying, Then God said, "Let Us make man in Our image, according to Our likeness; let them have dominion over the fish of the sea, over the birds of the air, and over the cattle, over all the earth and over every creeping thing that creeps on the earth." So God created man in His own image; in the image of God He created him; male and female He created them. Then God blessed them, and God said to them, "Be fruitful and multiply; fill the earth and subdue it; have dominion over the fish of the sea, over the birds of the air, and over every living thing that moves on the earth." (Gen 1:26-28). Here we see that God planned us to be made in His image. If we still are not sure about the identity and essence of God's image, God

Himself explains His image by saying, " ..In Our image...Our likeness..let them have dominion over..the sea...the air and on the earth". This image we can call it or phrase it as the 'dominion-image of God'.

The Hebrew word for dominion is 'radah' [pronounced rä·dä'] which means 1) to rule, have dominion, dominate, tread down a) (Qal) to have dominion, rule, subjugate b) (Hiphil) to cause to dominate 2) to scrape out a) (Qal) to scrape, scrape out. The dominion image of God is that heart in us which has the natural desire to rule over the surrounding in which we live. This 'dominion-image' is also the legal right given to man to rule over the entire earth, just as God rules over the entire universe. The Bible also confirms this by saying, "The heaven, even the heavens, are the LORD's [i.e. under His dominion]; But the [dominion of the] earth He has given to the children of men." (Ps 115:16).

But the problem is this dominion image of God will be active only as long as man is connected to God in his spirit-man. Because when God discussed about His

image, He did not speak in singularity but in plurality [i.e. He did not say 'I will create in My image' but He said, 'Let Us {which includes the Father, Son and the Holy Spirit} make man in Our image']. The strength of God lies in the role which each person of the trinity play to express His creative image of rulership, which He exercises over His Dominion. This is why God is three in person, but are one in purpose. This implies clearly that unless man is connected to God in his spirit with one purpose, he will not be able to express this dominion-image of God through his life. The power of Trinity lies in their unity. This unity can be defined as a dependency upon each other and a spirit connection of inter-penetration to one another. The Bible says, 'Now the Lord is the Spirit' (2 Cor 3:17). In other words, in this time-space bound now-realm of this earth, the Lord [i.e. God-connection in this earth] is the person of the Holy Spirit. It also means the one who works in us as Master over us and through us in this earth is the Holy Spirit. This dependency upon God the Spirit activates the dominion image of God in us. This dominion-image of God will give us unique identity and prominence because of the restoration of the original purpose of God in us. In other words we are wired and uniquely designed to fulfill this purpose. Praise the Lord!

God created man in His dominion-image, so that he can exercise dominion just like Him. Jesus was the one who first exhibited this exact dominion-image of God in this planet earth after the first Adam lost this image because of disobedience (1 Cor 15:45,49; Luke 3:38). For example Jesus said to the hypocritical religious leaders who opposed Jesus when He exercised dominion in the earth, "But if I cast out demons by the Spirit of God, surely the kingdom of God has come upon you." (Matt 12:28). In other words Jesus was telling them that the dominion image of God is what He was exercising and that is done by the Spirit of God Himself. In opposing the works of the Spirit of God who was working in Jesus these people were already opposing God's kingdom rule which has already come upon the earth through Jesus, which the Pharisees boasted as though they were the true representatives of it. In the succeeding verses Jesus spoke about their wrong critical and judgmental attitude in attributing the Spirit's work to the work of Satan, and that cannot be forgiven even for eternity because these religious people wanted to break the purpose of God which is to exercise the dominion-image of God in the planet earth (Matt 12:31-32). Jesus represented every one of us before God and he is the "repairer of the breach" (Is 58:12) or in other words the repairer of the lost God-connection of human kind.

Jesus also confirmed this reflection of God's dominion-image which he reflected by saying, "....Most assuredly, I say to you, the Son can do nothing of Himself, but what He sees the Father do; for whatever He does, the Son also does in like manner. For the Father loves the Son, and shows Him all things that He Himself does; and He will show Him greater works than these, that you may marvel" (John 5:19-20). Jesus also said "....the Father who dwells in Me does the works." (John 14:10). In other words, because of the spirit-connection Jesus had with God the Father, the works that Jesus did in this planet earth was equal to Father-God Himself sitting in the earthly body of Jesus and doing His works on earth. This spirit-connection to God through the Holy Spirit brings the dominion image of God in us to be activated to rule and reign in this planet earth (Eph 2:18). The power to rule and reign in this planet earth comes in to activation proportionately equal to the flow of communication between God and us. The more we are connected to God to represent God in His likeness, that much of power of authority and dominion image of God will be expressed on this earth.

The more we express it, the more prominent and unique identity we will have in God. This is the place where all the enemies of God in the spirit world will come to recognize the dominion image of God in us and through us, as the evil spirit himself confessed when it rebounded and attacked the faithless seven sons of Sceva, a Jewish Chief Priest, who had no God-connection [i.e. dominion-image of God] in their spirit man inside them (Acts 19:13-15). As the Bible says in Acts 19:15-16, "And the evil spirit answered and said, "Jesus I know, and Paul I know; but who are you?" Then the man in whom the evil spirit was leaped on them, overpowered them, and prevailed against them, so that they fled out of that house naked and wounded." Only when you are strong in your spirit-man with a mature dominion image of God inside you, all the principalities and powers will know you and will acknowledge the authority of God in you.

The dominion image of God was lost when Adam disobeyed God. The dominion over the world was in Adam's hand until the day "sin entered the world" (Rom 5:12). If we ask what is sin? The Bible says, "sin is lawlessness." (1 John 3:4). In other words sin is the lawless nature of the devil which acts against and rebels against God's dominion continuously (1 John 3:8). When the lawless nature of Satan began to influence humans legally in the soulish realm because of Adam's disobedience, all became sinners by an in-born nature of our soul (Rom 5:19). Adam's spirit connection to God became dead exactly on the day of his disobedience just exactly as God forewarned Adam (Gen 2:16-17). Once Adam's spirit connection to God was severed, Satan began to use his voice to direct man in the soulish realm because God has created the soul to be operative by spirit-direction. Jesus affirms this fact by saying that the believer will start to reject the voices of Satan and his demons, which He described as "the voice of strangers" (John 10:5). The more people get deceived by these spirit's voices in their soulish realm, the more they will become lawless. But the real voice of God will be heard by the believers because of a brand new spirit put within them by God to connect to Him (Ezek 36:26-27). These believers will begin to recognize the voice of God and He too will call them by name and will guide them as He had promised (John 10:3-4). The Spirit of God will be the one who will connect God's voice directly from His throne in heaven to our soul on earth. Our soul in turn will be able to recognize the voice of God on earth through our activated spirit within us (1 John 3:24; Heb 12:25; 1 Cor 2:10-12).

Hence for man to have dominion on the earth is closely interwoven with his dependency and God-connection that He experiences with God in his spirit, which is only revived, regenerated and renewed only for a born again believer in Christ Jesus (Eph 3:16; Tit 3:5; 2 Cor 4:16). So only Jesus said, ..."Most assuredly, I say to you, unless one is born of water and the Spirit, he cannot enter the kingdom of God. That which is born of the flesh is flesh, and that which is born of the Spirit is spirit." (John 3:5-6). In other words Jesus is saying only the Spirit of God can make the dead spirit of a human to be become connected to God's heavens life of the kingdom. Only those who are born from above can hear the voice of the wind which is the Holy Spirit of God (John 3:8).

The reason many people are oppressed more than ever in times past is because they do not accept and receive this truth of God [i.e. Jesus and His voice which is the Holy Spirit], rather they love to hear and receive deceptive soulish voices which will not be in-line with the truth of God revealed in the word of God (John 8:32; 2

Thess 2:9-12). The Apostle Paul in 2 Cor 4:4 says about these things clearly in his writing, "whose [i.e. unbeliever] minds the god of this age has blinded, who do not believe, lest the light of the gospel of the glory of Christ, who is the image of God, should shine on them." The dominion-image of God will shine on us as much as we believe to receive the light of the gospel of the glory of Christ. Until a person becomes hungry to hear the truth and receive it, he will never be able to differentiate between God's voice and the soulish voices he will hear in himself. This is the reason humans are not able to rule and reign in this planet earth, instead Satan and his evil cohort's bully people tyrannically and is ruling the world invisibly by promoting evil, destruction and peacelessness in this planet earth. Satan has been able to blind people's mind and deceive them is because man doesn't have the power to have dominion exercised without God. Man is wired in such a way, the one and only way he can exercise dominion on earth is by his oneness of purpose in his spirit, soul and body with God (Luke 1:37). Jesus himself humbly confessed this fact by saying, "I can of Myself do nothing...", even though he was the only begotten Son of God who came from heaven to this planet earth as an incarnated perfect substitute for every man (John 5:30; 3:16,17).

Satan and his evil cohorts are much more powerful as spirit beings than man, when man doesn't have that God-connection in himself through the Spirit of God. That's why the Apostle John wrote by Divine inspiration to the believers, "You are of God, little children, and have overcome them, because He who is in you [i.e. God the Holy Spirit] is greater than he who is in the world [i.e. Satan and his demons]." (1 John 4:4). In other words with God-connection in his spirit-man, man is more powerful that Satan and all his evil demons. This is confirmed in Ps 8:5-6 also, "For You have made him a little lower than the angels [i.e. Elohim.heb -> Creator God], and You have crowned him with glory and honor. You have made him to have dominion over the works of Your hands; You have [already] put all things [including the angels] under his feet..."

[Note: The meaning for the word 'Elohim' is exactly translated as God who is the Creator. But the Jewish tradition has wrongly translated it according to their tradition, calling God as angels just because they found the word to be pluralistic. But Christians have no problem in interpreting it as God the Creator in a pluralistic way because we know and believe the doctrine of trinity.]

Here we notice three things in these preceding verses,

1) By the purpose of God in the original creation of man, man is only a little lower than only the Creator God Himself.

2) The very purpose of making man is for him to have dominion.

3) God has already put all things under His feet [i.e. feet of Jesus Christ] and has seated us humans with Him in the heavenly places. Through this elevated standing we [i.e. men who are believers in Christ Jesus] are higher than the angels (Eph 1:18-23;

2:5-6). So only in the New Testament angels are exactly described in Heb 1:14 as, "Therefore, angels are only servants-spirits sent to care for people who will inherit salvation." [New Living Translation]. This has been confirmed by an angel himself who said, "See that you do not do that [i.e. fall down to worship me]. For I am your fellow servant, and of your brethren the prophets, and of those who keep the words of this book. Worship God." (Rev 22:9), when apostle John overawed by the prophetic words and visions that came from the angel on assignment, fell down to worship the angel.

To be close to God and to be powerful with dominion-image of God is the original purpose and intention of God for man in His original creation. This is still His will for every man in this planet earth (Rom 16:20). Satan didn't like the idea of God for him which is to be a guardian to man under him, so he rebelled against God's project of planet earth (Ezekiel 28:13-19). This is the reason Jesus taught His disciples to pray "Your kingdom come. Your will be done on earth as it is in heaven." (Matt

6:10) because Satan has rebelled against God and has been instigating and influencing men to act against God ever since the fall of first Adam. Only on earth God's will is not done because of Satan's evil influence over all men in this earth.

Man by God's creation purpose is custom built to exercise dominion by depending on God and having love relationship with Him. Human being only then will have perfect peace, love and unity to exercise dominion-image of God on the planet earth. Only this will give prominence and identity that every human longs for. Are you ready? You are asking me for what? To exercise God's dominion-image in this planet earth which is the sole purpose of our existence! Get that God-connection right and you will experience the dominion-image of God in you and through you. Praise the Lord!

DEATH HAS NO DOMINION OVER YOU

Are you afraid of death? Many people for fear of death have taken wrong steps and decisions, yet death has no power over a Christian believer, except he or she allows it. God promises to satisfy you with long life (Psalm 91:16) and to fulfill the number of your days (Exodus 23:26). This article seeks to free you from the fear of death and its consequences.

And release those who through fear of death were all their lifetime subject to bondage- Hebrews 2:15 (NKJV).

Now if we died with Christ, we believe that we shall also live with Him, knowing that Christ, having been raised from the dead, dies no more. Death no longer has dominion over Him - Romans 6:8-9 (NKJV).

Fear of death is a weapon with which the enemy has held many in bondage. Fear of death has caused many to follow the dictates of the devil. Also, people walk

about with fear of sudden attack because they are afraid of dying, and as such open the door for the enemy to attack them; for the scriptures say the following: fear has torments (1 John 4:18), your expectation shall not be cut off (Proverbs 23:18, KJV), as man thinks in his heart so is he (Proverbs 23:7), and you shall have what you say (Mark 11:23). When you expect negative things and confess the same, it won't be long for them to become realities in your life. You need to beware of this temptation to fear death and resist it!

Death the last thing to be destroyed (1 Corinthians 15:26) has no dominion over Christ, and anyone who receives Jesus as his personal Lord and Saviour also enjoys same victory- death has no dominion over him. Fear of death is of the devil but the fear of the Lord is life and it turns you from the snares of death (Proverbs 14:27). God has not given you the spirit of fear but of power, of love and of a sound mind (2 Timothy 1:7). You didn't receive the spirit of bondage again to fear, but of adoption so you can cry out "Abba Father" knowing that He is your Sun and Shield (Psalm

84:11), and your life is hidden with Christ in God (Colossians 3:3). Who then can touch you? If God be for you who can be against you? (Romans 8:31).

You need to know who you are in Christ and your position in Him and walk in that consciousness. You are seated in heavenly places in Christ Jesus far above principalities and powers (Ephesians 2:6, Ephesians 1:20-21). Though you live on earth, you are a citizen of heaven and have all the backings and protections of heaven. As such what is not obtainable in heaven is not permitted to manifest in your life.

Is it that you will live forever on earth? No, but that according to God's promise in the scriptures, you are to be satisfied with long life and that you will fulfill the number of your days. Anything short of this promise you are not to allow through sin or fear of death. You are to go about your daily business believing that no evil will befall you and that no plaque is permitted near your dwelling, a thousand may fall by your side but non shall come near you. In fact, you are to believe the fulfillment of Psalm 91 in your life.

Shadrach, Meshach, and Abed-nego in Daniel 3 had dominion over death. The furnace that killed others could not kill them because they knew who they were in God and believed in God's ability to deliver them. They didn't give in to the fear of death and so did not take the wrong decision; rather they choose to obey God. Also, Daniel had dominion over death. They threw him into the lion's den but the lions couldn't eat him, but when those who conspired against him were thrown in, the lions had a great feast (Daniel 6). Daniel overcame because he didn't allow fear of death to stop him from serving his God. And God proved Himself faithful in his life.

Furthermore, Paul manifested a great dominion over death. In Acts 14:19-20, certain Jews persuaded some people to stone Paul, after which they cast him outside the city thinking he was dead, but he got up and left the city alive. To crown it all, he reached a point where he was between the desire to live or to depart and

be with Christ (Philippians 1:21-26). Paul was a child of God like you, and God has not changed. The difference is that Paul believed God's word totally and trusted in the Lord to do what He said He will do.

Therefore, whatever may be happening around you, no matter what you see or hear, don't give in to fear of death, instead believe God to fulfill Psalm 91 totally in your life. Don't open the door through sin, and your testimony will be like Paul's testimony. May God satisfy you with long life and fulfill your number of days in Jesus name.

REASONS WHY WE NEED TO HAVE PERMANENT DOMINION OVER FEAR

Fear is a negative feeling which can lead to worry and anxiety in the life of an individual. There are two major categories of fear: Godly Fear and Ungodly Fear. Dominion on the other hand implies the ability to have control or to be in charge of a situation. It can also be defined as the having power to overcome a situation. In this article, I will be focusing on the several reasons why we need to have dominion over ungodly fear.

God has not given us the spirit of fear

One of the fundamental truth we must all understand, is that God has not given us the spirit of fear, but of boldness, sound mind and of love. What this means, is that fear is not part of what has been deposited in our life. It is an external influence from the devil which must not be allowed to stay. We all know that fear can steal, kill and destroy our joy and happiness in life.

as we begin to exercise boldness and a sound mind, fear will disappear!

it is not in the character of lions to be afraid

In my years on earth, I have never seen a lion running away from a sheep. It is the other way around. The lion is one of the most fearless animals in the animal kingdom. A small cub is born with the dominion mentality, which will not allow any animal to intimidate him/her. It is in their gene, and it flows from generation to generation. Jesus who is our perfect example is the lion of the tribe of Judah, and as little Christ, we are more like little cubs. A measure of his dominion mentality has been imputed in us immediately we became born again. All we need to do to begin to operate in the realm of dominion is to activate it in faith.

whatever we are afraid of, will turn around to haunt us later

If we are afraid of sickness, the body chemistry will attract sickness into our life. If we afraid of Mathematics and we keep finding way to avoid it in class, it will someday come over to haunt us. We must confront our fear and deal with it once and for all. The ☐uestion we must ask ourselves is: "why must I run away from my fears?". There is absolutely no reason why we must run away. It is like postponing the evil day.

Fear can destroy our dream and destiny in life

All the resources we need to succeed in life has been made available to us by God. Unfortunately, some individual are too afraid to make use of their gift and talent. In the book of Matthew 25:14-28, we are told the story of a master who shared talents to three of his servants. One of the servant who was given one talent, decided to hide his talent beneath the earth, because of fear. The master eventually returned and expressed displeasure with his action. The one talent was taken away from him and given to the servant who had five talent. This implies that God expects us to be productive and use our talents and gifts to achieve our dreams and destiny in life. there are individuals who are potential Grammy award winners hiding in church congregation because of fear of failure. The moment we break loose of every fear holding us stagnant, our dreams will come alive.

God is with us always

This is one of the most precious promises te lord has given to his children on earth. As Jesus was about to ascend to heaven he promised that he will not leave us comfortless, but that he will send the Holy Spirit to comfort and direct us daily. Hear what he has to say: "though I walk through the valley of the shadow of death, I shall fear no evil: for God is with me". The assurance of his everlasting presence is capable of destroying every trace of fear in our life. In the day or night, he has promised to be with us. As we travel in the air, on land or in the sea, he is always there.

Christ has conquered our fear

When Jesus Christ died on the cross of Calvary, he conquered all our fear and made a public shame of it. Therefore fear does not have dominion over our live anymore. There is a greater power in you, that is bigger than that of all your fears combined together. Having a clear knowledge of this awesome power will set you free from all your fears. He has conquered fear on our behalf and has given us power to tread upon our fears.

We have overcome through the blood

The precious blood of the lamb is an antidote to all fear that has been plaguing our life. One reason why we must not be afraid is because we have overcome our fear by the blood of the lamb. Not just the blood alone, but by the living word of God. For every fear that comes our way, the blood has a solution. The word of God also has an answer. The potent power of the blood is capable of neutralizing the twin agents of fear and anxiety.

CALLED TO CONQUER

Romans 8:37-39. Yet in all these things we are more than conquerors through Him who loved us. For I am persuaded that neither death nor life, nor angels nor principalities nor powers, nor things present nor things to come, nor height nor depth, nor any other created thing, shall be able to separate us from the love of God which is in Christ Jesus our Lord.

The Greek Word for conqueror here is hupernikao. Vines New Testament dictionary says that hupernikao is to gain a surpassing victory, lit., "we are hyper-conquerors," i.e., we are pre-eminently victorious.

We are not just conquerors (nikao) we are much more, we are super conquerors (hupernikao). WOW.

This may come as a revelation to many Christians, but we are not supposed to be punching bags for the devil, this is not what God called us to be. He called us to

be con□uerors and to walk in victory over every adversity. Many Christians pray and ask God to please take away the problems of life, they just don't realize that God has e□uipped us to do it. We are to walk in the victory that has been bought for us. The Word of God has a lot to say about this, and not just in the New Testament, this is a recurring theme through the whole Bible.

It started in the garden of Eden. Genesis 1:28. Then God blessed them, and God said to them, "Be fruitful and multiply; fill the earth and subdue it; have dominion over the fish of the sea, over the birds of the air, and over every living thing that moves on the earth."

God told Adam to subdue and also to have dominion over all the Earth. Adam was given great authority. He had the legal rights to this planet, yet he gave those rights over to Satan.
It was not until the second Adam, Jesus, that we were able to receive back what was originally given to Adam, this authority was legally purchased back and given to us.

Thousands of years later, Jesus came, but before He started His earthly ministry He was led into the wilderness by the Holy Spirit to be tempted by Satan.

Matthew, Mark and Luke all have accounts of this. Jesus had to go through real temptation and overcome many things before He could start His ministry here on Earth. We have got to understand that Jesus had choices to make or it would not have been a real temptation.

The first thing that Jesus did was submit to God and be baptized, at this time God anointed Him with the Holy Spirit to do service. The second thing He did was to make a declaration of His mission. He declared why He was sent.

Luke 4:18 "The Spirit of the Lord is upon Me, because He has anointed Me to preach the gospel to the poor. He has sent Me to heal the brokenhearted, to preach deliverance to the captives and recovery of sight to the blind, to set at liberty those who are oppressed,

19. to preach the acceptable year of the Lord."

Jesus was sent by God the Father to heal broken hearts, deliver the captives, recover sight for the blind, and to liberate the oppressed, and to preach the acceptable year of the Lord.
The acceptable year of the Lord was the year of jubilee. This was the year of restoration for the Jew's, when houses and lands were restored, slaves were set free, and restitution was made.

Jesus made it plain this is what He came to do, to free us, to liberate us. He came to restore what was taken. He was called to conquer. I would like to ask you the question, has He changed even a little bit? No He has not, however Satan is still the God of this world.

Jesus gave us instructions before He left, He told us to ...
Mark 16:15-20. And He said to them, "Go into all the world and preach the gospel to every creature. He who believes and is baptized will be saved; but he who does not believe will be condemned. And these signs will follow those who believe: In My

name they will cast out demons; they will speak with new tongues; they will take up serpents; and if they drink anything deadly, it will by no means hurt them; they will lay hands on the sick, and they will recover." So then, after the Lord had spoken to them, He was received up into heaven, and sat down at the right hand of God. And they went out and preached everywhere, the Lord working with them and confirming the word through the accompanying signs. Amen.

Jesus has commissioned us to carry on the work in His name. He transferred His authority to us. He called us to con□uer. Jesus has restored the authority that Adam lost in the garden of Eden, but many believers are ignorant of the authority that they truly have. We have to learn to walk in this authority by exercising our faith in the Word of God. Religion says no, and has taught us to be mealy bug Christians, just barely getting along. However that is not what God's Word says. Jesus told his disciples to go, however before they could go they were told ...

Acts 1:8 But you shall receive power when the Holy Spirit has come upon you; and you shall be witnesses to Me in Jerusalem, and in all Judea and Samaria, and to the end of the earth.

Just as Jesus had to have God's anointing, so He gave the Holy Spirit to His disciples to carry out His commission. They had to wait for the Holy Spirit before they could begin to carry out God's great commission didn't they?
As we step out in faith and go, we will also grow in grace and knowledge. There is a learning process here, as we go we grow. However we are not on our own.

Jesus said ...
John 16:13 "However, when He, the Spirit of truth, has come, He will guide you into all truth; for He will not speak on His own authority, but whatever He hears He will speak; and He will tell you things to come.

The enemy is still here and very real. That is the thing about being a con□ueror, you're not a conqueror if you don't have an enemy to conquer are you? How are we going to be super conquerors as the Word of God says when we are the ones who are always begging God to take us out of every bad situation that pops up? I'm not saying bad situations are fun, I'm saying we have a purpose on this Earth to stand up in the authority that Jesus purchased back legally for us and to do something about the problem. Jesus dealt with problems every step of the way, He fought devils and sickness every step of the way. He fought religious bigotry every step of the way. He was not here asking God to deliver Him from the sickness disease and spiritual death that was all around Him, He was sent to do something about these things. He was sent to conquer these things. He was here to destroy the works of Satan.

1 John 3:8. He who sins is of the devil, for the devil has sinned from the beginning. For this purpose the Son of God was manifested, that He might destroy the works of the devil.

This is the whole purpose of being a conqueror, to destroy the works of the devil. To overcome every adversity that

Satan throws our way. This is not just for our benefit but for the benefit of the whole world. This is the message we carry, we have been given the message of reconciliation to God, and it is our job to share this good news with the world.
We have to receive the revelation of God's Word and realize that beggars and paupers are not con□uerors!!! This is just exactly what we are called to do, to subdue the Earth and have dominion over it. We are not talking about conquering land masses but the physical and spiritual oppression of the enemy. If there was no enemy there would be no conquerors, We would have nothing to con□uer. We would just be inhabititors. We have been called to walk as children of God and to walk in the authority Jesus has given to us. Jesus said...

Luke 10:19 "Behold, I give you the authority to trample on serpents and scorpions, and over all the power of the enemy, and nothing shall by any means hurt you.

This authority has been given to us by the Lord Jesus Christ, but it does us no good if we will not learn to walk in it, and to also take this message to others.

2 Corinthians 5:18-21. Now all things are of God, who has reconciled us to Himself through Jesus Christ, and has given us the ministry of reconciliation, that is, that God was in Christ reconciling the world to Himself, not imputing their trespasses to them, and has committed to us the word of reconciliation. Therefore we are ambassadors for Christ, as though God were pleading through us: we implore you on Christ's behalf, be reconciled to God. For He made Him who knew no sin to be sin for us, that we might become the righteousness of God in Him.

This is truly the good news of the Gospel, and we are the ones sent to declare the freedom in Jesus Christ. We have to declare Jesus can heal broken hearts, deliver the captives, recover sight for the blind, and to liberate the oppressed, and we have to declare the year of jubilee is here, now!!!!!! If you have never thought about yourself like a super conqueror then I would like to for you to take stock and begin to see yourself through the eyes of God's Word. Amen.

I would like to invite you to take the first step if you haven't already, and meet the Lord Jesus Christ for yourself. The first step to know for sure that you are a child of God, is to earnestly pray this prayer.

In this study I would like to talk about the purpose for our being conquerors. Have you ever stopped to consider the reason for us being called to conquer? Jesus has already defeated Satan, yet he is still in this world and he still has power. However his authority has been taken away. He no longer has the authority to use that power, we are the spiritual police that have been placed here to enforce God's plan for this Earth.

Jesus said in Luke 10:19. "Behold, I give you the authority to trample on serpents and scorpions, and over all the power of the enemy, and nothing shall by any means hurt you.

This is the New king James version. The original King James said behold I give you power.
The correct translation here is authority as the New King James says it. Vines says authority means... From the meaning of "leave or permission," or liberty of doing as one pleases, it passed to that of "the ability or strength with which one is endued," then to that of the "power of authority," the right to exercise power, also the power of rule or government," the power of one whose will and commands must be obeyed by others, that which is subject to authority or rule, one who possesses authority, a ruler, magistrate.

In other words Jesus said we were given the right to command and exercise power over the enemy. He is the One who has given us this authority. We were given very specific authority for a purpose. Without the authority to use God's power we would fail in our mission here. However God has not called us to fail. We are called to con□uer. As we said in the first study, if there was no enemy we would not need to be a conqueror. I realize this sounds like an obvious statement, but it is a truth that much of the body of Christ has not seen. If there was no obstacle to overcome, God would not have needed to give us the ability to overcome would He??? He has given us the authority to overcome and has done so, so that we can fulfill our purpose here on this Earth, to fulfill the great commission.

Jesus said we are the salt of the Earth, what good is salt if it has lost its saltiness. It's no good at all. We are here to preserve this Earth, not just to take up space. We do this by walking in the authority that Jesus has given to us. We are here to enforce what Jesus has already accomplished. We are here to take back by the power of God what Satan is illegally taking from God's children. That's the reason for the authority. Not just so there would be no problems. There are always going to be problems. We have been called to enforce God's rule and overcome every problem so that the Gospel can go forth over the Earth.

But first of all we have to understand that there is a process to this. We don't start out as walking as world conquerors, even though we have been given the authority we have to learn to walk in these things. We start out as babies. We have to learn to walk in this victory so that we can keep and preserve the land that we have overcome, and not loose what we have gained. I have seen people delivered by the power of God and then some months later loose what they had received. The reason for this is that they had no teaching on how to keep the victory. They did not know how to walk in a sustained state of victory and maintain what they had been given. They lost what was legally theirs. They still had the authority to stay delivered, but they didn't know how to walk in it. God wants us to con□uer the land progressively and keep what we have won. It's hard to take the victory away from someone who has con□uered the land and fortified the walls after they inhabited it. On the other hand if they had just walked into the land and pitched a tent, they would be ripe for the enemies picking so to speak.

The Old Testament is full of such examples and they are there for our benefit. We can see how the children of Israel succeeded and also failed if they didn't follow God's plan.

1 Corinthians 10:11 Now all these things happened to them as examples, and they were written for our admonition, on whom the ends of the ages have come.
Let's take a look at an Old Testament example of this.

Exodus 23:27-30. "I will send My fear before you, I will cause confusion among all the people to whom you come, and will make all your enemies turn their backs to you.
And I will send hornets before you, which shall drive out the Hivite, the Canaanite, and the Hittite from before you. I will not drive them out from before you in one year, lest the land become desolate and the beast of the field become too numerous for you. Little by little I will drive them out from before you, until you have increased, and you inherit the land.

We can see God's intent here in this passage of Scripture. His sole purpose all along was for them to occupy the land and not loose it. He didn't call them into the desert to fail, but because they would not accept that, and were disobedient and not trusting, they had to die off first before a new generation could come in and inherited the promised land.

These people of God were never able to inherit the promised land because they refused to put their trust in Him.

They were called to the land that they were to inherit. They were called to the land that they were to con□ueror. God did all the work and they got the promise, yet they had a part to play in this. They had to trust God, and walk in obedience. We also see that it didn't happen all at once for a very good reason. It happened gradually so that the land would not become desolate, and be taken over by the beasts of the field. You don't have to strain very hard in order to see the New Testament correlation in this.

God went before them and drove out the enemy, then He walked the children of

Israel into their land in such a way that they would be able to keep it, and sustain it. Little by little.

The children of Israel had to inhabit the land as they conquered it. There was a process to fulfilling God's plan. God ordains growth this way, least we loose the victory. God always has a purpose for us to con□uer the land and we must follow His directions in order to succeed. God has ordained us to conquer our enemies. He has also called us to con□uer the circumstances that would get in the way of what He has called us to do. We have all had circumstances in life that have seemed to overwhelm us at times yet God has called us to walk through them victoriously, not die in them. The children of Israel were led into the wilderness into very adverse circumstances, an estimated 3 to 4 million people with no food or water. They would not consider that God had not delivered them out of the bondage of slavery in Egypt, to give them a new life. They murmured and complained against Moses all the time. There are 11 different Scriptures making mention of this in the

Old Testament. God had a plan and a purpose all along if they would have just trusted Him. Murmuring and complaining will only defeat you in life. As I have already stated, God did not call them into the wilderness to die, yet that is just what happened because of their murmuring and complaining, and their thankless attitude.

1 Corinthians 10:9-10 nor let us tempt Christ, as some of them also tempted, and were destroyed by serpents; nor murmur, as some of them also murmured, and were destroyed by the destroyer.

Murmuring and complaining will only open the door to the enemy and gives him an opportunity to thwart the plan and purpose of God in your life, again, this was never God's will for them. God led them through a series of circumstances to teach them to trust in Him, not to destroy them. They were given the opportunity to learn to trust in Him. This was a time of preparation. Have you ever considered that they would have never con☐uered the promised land if they had not learned to trust in God first? It was through all the wilderness experiences that they truly got this opportunity. They were constantly surrounded by enemies as well as adverse circumstances that seemed to say you can't succeed, yet God delivered them out of them all!!!!! There is a lesson here for us all. The Lord is our complete resource, yet we have to come to acknowledge His total provision. Let's learn from their experiences.

Let's look at our opening Scripture again, Romans 8:37-39. Yet in all these things we are more than conquerors through Him who loved us. For I am persuaded that neither death nor life, nor angels nor principalities nor powers, nor things present nor things to come, nor height nor depth, nor any other created thing, shall be able to separate us from the love of God which is in Christ Jesus our Lord.

We have to learn as the children of Israel did, to put our trust in Him. As conquerors we have to come to the place where we put our total trust in God, or we will never conquer the land as our Lord intended.

Proverbs 3:5-6. Trust in the Lord with all your heart, and lean not on your own understanding; in all your ways acknowledge Him, and He shall direct your paths.

God is faithful, we must praise him in every circumstance of life, not for every circumstance but in every circumstance. He is all sufficient to meet our every need regardless of what is thrown our way. The children of Israel would not put away their slave mentality and place their trust in God. He can be trusted. Lift up your eyes, we serve the one true God who is more than sufficient in every circumstance of life.

Lets look at the commission the Lord Jesus Himself gave us before He departed this Earthly realm.

Matthew 28:18-20. Then Jesus came and spoke to them, saying, "All authority has been given to Me in heaven and on earth. Go therefore and make disciples of all the nations, baptizing them in the name of the Father and of the Son and of the Holy

Spirit, teaching them to observe all things that I have commanded you; and lo, I am with you always, even to the end of the age.'' Amen.''

The great focus of the modern church has been to go and get people born into the kingdom. This is certainly an important first step, but that is not what Jesus said to do. He said to make disciples of all the Nations, also teaching them to observe all the things that He commanded. Lately, I have come to see this in a new light. A nation can be won to Christ but not discipled. This is a nation that can be lost as quickly as it was won. There are some real examples of this in history. The great Welsh revival of the early 1900's transformed a nation, however approximately 100 years later, less than two percent of the nation goes to church. The impact the revival had on that nation was in itself unprecedented in modern history. However, the long lasting affects of the revival were not sustained. Regardless of the move of God, we have to look ahead through God's eyes and see not just what He is doing, but where He is wanting to go. He always has a purpose for what He does.

God doesn't start things just to see them die out. It doesn't have to be that way. We have been given the authority to do what He told us to do.

Think about this, Adam was given dominion over the whole Earth. Consider the implications of what that means. Man was given the ability, the desire, and the authority to walk in total dominion upon this planet. We still have this innate desire within ourselves to want to control and dominate. All you have to do is look at the mess the world is in, and you can see this for yourself. New threats of nuclear disaster are popping up every day. Nations are threating to annihilate one another. To want to control and dominate outside of the plan and purpose of God is a very dangerous thing. However, with God and within His purpose, it is the destiny we have been called to fulfill through Christ Jesus.

The authority Adam lost has been restored. Jesus said "All authority has been given to Me in heaven and on earth. Go therefore. The authority has been given to me, and I am turning that authority over to you, therefor go out and make disciples of all nations. It seems Christianity has become just another religion who co-exist with everyone else. Nobody wants to offend anyone, so in the wake of political correctness we just roll over and play religion. I realize this is a harsh statement. It is not meant to offend, but to be a wake up call, and to make us realize we have a job to do.

If you have spent any time in the Old Testament you will see that here are examples for us to follow, types and shadows of what we are supposed to be. The children of Israel would not trust God, and cross into the promised land that God had ordained for them to conquer. This was a serious thing. God still loved them and took care of them. He blessed them as much as they would let Him, yet this was far below what He wanted for them. They became used to it, and their carcasses died in the wilderness. God wanted to bless them and He could not. They refused the blessing. When you are willfully disobedient to God, you refuse the blessing He wants you to have whether you realize it or not. If you look at the parallel of the modern church, you can see this same attitude. We haven't dared to step over into what God has called us to be. In some circles if you dare step out and declare that God has given you the land, and you say that God wants me blessed and prosperous, you would be called arrogant and greedy. Many would say just who do they think they are anyway? Many have backed away from their destiny because they didn't want to cross that line, never fully considering that it is a line that God called them to cross over. If the devil can make you think you are not worthy to cross over into your inheritance, then he has won the battle without even having to fight.

Lets look at the second generation of the children of Israel that actually went over into the promised land. A land of milk and honey, a land of prosperity, a land that God ordained for them to live in. This is a type of what God wants for us, to conquer and inhabit our God ordained place, our place of prosperity. He does not want us to lay down and die in the wilderness. That was not His will for the first generation and that is not His will for us now in this present generation. The second generation started out with a completely different attitude than the first generation had. Lets look at how they started out.

Joshua 1:16 And they answered Joshua, saying, "All that you command us we will do, and wherever you send us we will go. 17. "Just as we heeded Moses in all things, so we will heed you. Only the Lord your God be with you, as He was with Moses.

They started out with the affirmation, we will follow God wherever he will send us.

Quite a different attitude than the one the first generation had wasn't it? Under Joshua's leadership, the children of Israel began to systematically take the land. They con□uered it, then they also inhabited it, and in doing so they fulfilled God's will. If you read through the book of Joshua, you can see how important it was for them to con□uer the land and inhabit it. Joshua actually scolded some of them for not aggressively doing what they were told to do.

Joshua 18:2-3 But there remained among the children of Israel seven tribes which had not yet received their inheritance. Then Joshua said to the children of Israel: "How long will you neglect to go and possess the land which the Lord God of your fathers has given you?

Joshua said that God had already given them the land, yet they didn't take it to heart and actually possess the land that God had given them. Joshua called this negligence. When you don't possess your God given inheritance you are being negligent, and this is a form of disobedience. Throughout the Bible, the people of God who were the most successful were not always necessarily the most perfect ones, but they were the ones who fulfilled God's will. King David was certainly not perfect, but he was somebody who fulfilled God's assignment. God highly blessed Him for His obedience. You will see this over and over again. When people put

God's kingdom assignment first, God blesses them.

Deuteronomy 8:18 "And you shall remember the Lord your God, for it is He who gives you power to get wealth, that He may establish His covenant which He swore to your fathers, as it is this day.

The word of God said this of David...

Acts 13:22 "And when He had removed him, He raised up for them David as king, to whom also He gave testimony and said, `I have found David the son of Jesse, a man after My own heart, who will do all My will.'

Even though David messed up, his desire was to complete the mission God had given him and fulfill God's will. Its not how big of a ministry you build or how well known you are, but did you fulfill God's will? This is a ◻uestion we each have to ask ourselves, what is God's will for my life? We each have a God given place, God wants us to inhabit the land he has called us to. Our blessing is in the land He has called us to inhabit. We can't get our God ordained blessing going south if God has called us to go north. If you want to prosper, then you have to be obedient. Thats the way it works. If you can enlarge your vision a little, you can take a little more. The bigger the vision the more you can take.

Joshua 17:14-18 Then the children of Joseph spoke to Joshua, saying, "Why have you given us but one lot and one portion to inherit, since we are a great people, inasmuch as the Lord has blessed us until now?" So Joshua answered them, If you are a great people, then go up to the forest country and clear a place for yourself there in the land of the Perizzites and the giants, since the mountains of Ephraim are too confined for you. But the children of Joseph said, "The mountain country is not enough for us; and all the Canaanites who dwell in the land of the valley have chariots of iron, both those who are of Beth Shean and its towns and those who are of the Valley of Jezreel. And Joshua spoke to the house of Joseph to Ephraim and Manasseh saying, You are a great people and have great power; you shall not have one lot only, but the mountain country shall be yours. Although it is wooded, you shall cut it down, and its farthest extent shall be yours; for you shall drive out the Canaanites, though they have iron chariots and are strong.

Joshua didn't say well you greedy little buggers, don't you know God doesn't want you to have all that land, just who do you think you are anyway? No, and God didn't get angry with them either. Joshua said go for it. You can do it. Take what you need. You can surely conquer the land!

I pray this Scripture in Isaiah takes on some new meaning now.

Isaiah 1:19 If you are willing and obedient, you shall eat the good of the land;

Are you willing? The next step is obedience, so go for it, and be a man or woman after God's own heart, and do all His will. Inhabit your promised land. Amen

Do you know Jesus as your Lord and Savior? Do you want to be a joint heir with Christ?

If so, I urge you to earnestly pray the following prayer.

Dear Heavenly Father, I come to you in the name of Jesus. Your word says, "and the one who comes to Me I will by no means cast out." (Jn.6:37),

So I know You won't cast me out, but You take me in, And I thank you for it. You said in your Word, "whoever calls upon the name of the Lord shall be saved." (Ro. 10:13).

I am calling on Your name, So I know You have saved me now, You also said, "that if you confess with your mouth the Lord Jesus and believe in your heart that God has raised Him from the dead, you will be saved. For with the heart one believes to righteousness, and with the mouth confession is made to salvation." (Ro.10:9,10).

I believe in my heart that Jesus Christ is the Son of God. I believe He was raised from the dead for my justification. And I confess Him now as my Lord, Because Your Word says, " with the heart one believes to righteousness" and I do believe with my heart, I have now become the righteousness of God in Christ. (2 Cor. 5:21),

And I am saved! Thank You, Lord!

I can now truthfully say, I see myself as a born again child of God!